1985

Fish, Flesh, & Fowl

Fish, Flesh, & Fowl

Poems by

WILLIAM HATHAWAY

Louisiana State University Press

Baton Rouge and London   1985

Designer: Albert Crochet
Typeface: Linotron Century Schoolbook
Typesetter: G & S Typesetters, Inc.
Printer and binder: Edwards Brothers, Inc.

Some of these poems have appeared in the following
magazines: *American Poetry Review, Atlanta, Chiaroscuro,
Cimarron Review, Crazyhorse, Greenfield Review, Hudson
Review, Kansas Quarterly, Kenyon Review, Manchac,
Midwest Quarterly, New England Review, New Letters,
Ploughshares, Poetry, Poetry East, Poetry Miscellany, Poetry
Now, Sidewinder, South & West, Telescope, Texas Review.*

Library of Congress Cataloging in Publication Data

Hathaway, William, 1944–
  Fish, flesh, & fowl.

  I. Title. II. Title: Fish, flesh, and fowl.
PS3558.A75F5   1985   811'.54   84-23332
ISBN 0-8071-1233-X
ISBN 0-8071-1232-1 (pbk.)

To Sherry Hathaway

Contents

Fish, Flesh, & Fowl

The Iceball

Mittens tucked fat in my armpit,
I packed it harder and harder to ice
in bare hands. My outraged blood
blazed rosepetal-pink through the skin
of my palms. This one I meant
to throw with all my might
at Larry Darrah's head when they charged.
Anonymous in the arcing blizzard
of snowballs, this one would speed
deadly true to knock his god damn eye
out of his ugly face. Because Darrah
was a cruel prick, that was my scheme.

This bomb was too beautiful: ball-
bearing round, smoother than a crystal
globe, of heft so perfect my arm *knew*
it could not miss, but could not let it go.
I cached it in a niche of our snowfort
to juggle it home in my bare hands
so red yarn from my mittens would not
fuzz it up. O, it was too good for Darrah!
This iceball transcended craft to hold
its own absolute light—a fierce sparkle
too pure for any enemy I knew.

When I took it from the freezer
on the big scorcher in late July
one side had flattened and rough frost
furred its once-slick curves.
The clear glisten had clouded to milky
dun; it had shrunk and smelled
like stale food. Yes, it was interesting
to see it sweat so fast into a cold
puddle on hot cement, how geometric
crystals clung and clarified
in their final blaze. But in those coils
below my stomach where things turn
really disgusting I felt regret—
a miser's loss clogging the pipes.

Ah, that Larry Darrah. He walked ram-
rod straight, like a coke bottle
filled his poop-chute. He chewed
tobacco just to spit it on my pants
and he washed my face with snow
many times, in front of lots of girls.
Teachers loved him and said he was
likely to be elected president one day.
The day I did not knock his damn eye
out was the first time I let this country
down.

A Crush

Do—Re—Me—Fa—So—Thunk!
Do—re—mi—fa—so—La—La—la-ti-do.
As if late August sun could not set
without the pitiless descent and climb
of those dismal rungs, her little brother
played our porch song nightly.

Whenever piano scales reach me, from high
curtain-waving windows or echoing halls
of sedate purpose, I smell that meatloaf
from the black screen door with its feeble
television moon. Because when those dull notes
ceased, a cicada's drone from a tall elm's
droop took up that keen of dolor
and despair, until its whine was cut off
so hard before its natural peak, dusk
suddenly just hung in unabated yearning.
I wince at the memory of my high-pitched
jabber—a plea sobbing in every syllable.

For I adored the soft down rippling on
her jaw when she chewed gum. She loved
the lifeguard at the country club. Tab Hunter
hair, ivy-league smirk and blazer; he dropped
full-blown from birth in a red convertible
onto our town's sleepy streets, like Hercules
serving a casual summer's penance. Certainly
a monotonous clang of horseshoes from distant
lawns never tugged a discordant ache in *his*
fresh heart. I loathed my skinny arms in short-
sleeves, my timid, sweet-cheeping soul.

If the evening breeze carried his car horn's wolf-
whistle from far-off avenues to where we slumped
on her porch stoop, a flickering luster cleared
blue fathoms in her eyes. God, how my teeth
needed to bite the pout of her lower lip!

But one night beneath buzzing streetlamps, I
kicked a soup can home and never did go back.
I don't know why. The clankey-clank-
clank of that can had an angry ring I liked—
more my kind of song than the dreamy moans
of trains that got Dick Nixon scheming in *his* bed.
I knew what those blade-thin beams from parted drapes
on crewcut lawns wished for me: a depression, a good
war for a boy who yipped back at their unchained dogs.

Late and Early Geese

More often they pass over as ragged checkmarks
than those balanced vees of tradition.
The route's still north/south and sunsets
are sloppier, more paprika swirling in the sour
cream, than ever—what with the Mexican
volcano. A cartoon made me wonder why
their formation's never vertical, a stately V
for victory strut, derisive honks and a small
confetti rain of ejectamenta in its wake.
Sure makes you wonder how the shining Cross
positioned itself for Constantine, or if
those show jets buzzing the anthem at the Rose
Bowl are imitating nature. Well, it's quite
obvious. Sergeant Alvin York beaded over
twenty Huns, lined in a trench, on the lead-
bird principle. He got religion in a lightning
storm, just like Luther, and Gary Cooper
did a bang-up job playing him. But what
can a checkmark ever mean but "OK, right.
I gotcha"? We seem to greet these signs
of seasons' passage with more relief
than triumph lately, but their far calls
in early February startled me. I thought
some babies were locked and left like pups
in some cold parked car. But there they were,
such sad, insistent bleats. Over Myer's Point,
they banked east to circle once again our
bare, gray squares, white and brown in patches.
And because I knew that didn't mean a thing
beyond a second look, I knew it meant no good.

Why That's Bob Hope

The comedian, holding a chunk of flaming shale.
If only *Der Bingle* could see him now! He looked
so puffed and sleepy in that Texaco hardhat,
I could've popped a fuse. Well, like the oil,

here today and gone today. In *my* good old days
Hope was on Sullivan's "shew" so often us kids
dropped TV for longhair sex and smoking weeds.
What a mistake! But now we're past our wild phase

and Bob's back with this burning rock, funny
for a change. No, no old quips now about Dean's double
vision, Phyllis Diller's breasts, or Sinatra's aging treble.
He says if we all squeeze the rock together real money

will drip out. We'll live real good and still afford a war
where he'll bust our boys' guts on tour in El Salvador.

Tardiness Lecture

for my son Jesse

On my knees in the powdered dust
covering packed dirt under the see-saw
I put my face close to the earth
to watch two ants grapple to the death
of both. Ants were ants to me,
but one had an abdomen of burnished
copper, the other was all black, so I
guessed they held some ancient grudge.

Jaws locked at a fulcrum, they strained
and teetered in most serious silence
until the red one suddenly crumpled
into a still and curled thing. I was
a God. Indifferent, benign, I watched
the other limp some inches off, topple
on its remaining legs and also die.

When I raised my head back up
to my own world, vast and brilliant,
it was to terror. For only
the wind tumbled leaves and paper
scraps across the quiet playground.
My school seemed to hum like a bomb,
a busy beebox, from its yellow windows
as I stumbled on strange legs to my fate.
My tongue was a dry stick in a dusty
crevice: useless in my defense.

She made me stand before the class
and jabbed her pointer at my head.
I could not contain my tears. Nor
can I remember what words spat out
of her writhing lips, but to this day
I always stiffen just a bit
when I hear that word "tardy" said.
Some meanly grinned, while others tried
with all their might to see the swirl
of woodgrain at the centers of their desks.
All through that longest day I longed
to blow my nose in the soft folds
of our nobly drooping flag, sharing
that public corner where she put me.

And now, in discourse, what lesson
can I give to you? For that is the serious
mode, it is supposed. That it is an insect's
life, fraught with struggle; we must submit?
Or will resistance (though it is a Sin)
at least bring dignity to recompense the pain?
Critics' questions. Which I do not disdain,
but these fools mark time with petty bells
and you had best obey, my boy—or else.

Watching the Fishing Show

The best part is when, trout or bass,
it hits the lure. While the pole
does its crazy pointing, like a bird-
dog following its dripping tongue,
or a dowser's rod in Oklahoma,
everything gets in balance. I mean
the pull on arms, shoulders, and back
exactly matches the give of water
cushioning the boat. Ancient Greeks
referred to this in different contexts.

But you must rush to turn off the sound
or the sportsman's bluff monologue,
a whisper sneering like the tough boy's
joke in church, will wreck it all.
He says "Beauty" often, but the way
the uncle who kept punching your arm
did, staring at your mother's behind.

The very best part is when silver
flashes wink back and forth next to
the boat and the tail begins to rip
little holes in the lake. You are
about to pull part of yourself up
into yourself. Hypnotized by its zig-
zag, you might murmur "hither,
thither, and yon" to your own mind.
Who knows why? These words sound
like "winken, blinken, and nod."

When the fish is boated, expertly
measured, and held up for the sun
to see, it is over. You become
as bored as their sober guide looks.
But it's not over! No matter
you've seen it hundreds of times,
it flabbergasts you as they release
the fish into the bouncing wrinkles,
slip it free with a careless flourish!

If you could catch such fish,
so many, so big—your wife
would come home from her sad religion.
Your children would quit drugs
to honor you, but to these beefy sports,
easy in their wealth of orange flesh
it is *por nada*. *Sprezzatura*: a big wink,
fat hand on your back, some dollars
stuffed in your shirtpocket. Let's
face it, nothing has been the same
since Momma brought the new baby home
from the hospital and that fish
could make all the difference.

Carp

Like a great gray hand
of a dying emperor, let's say,
dismissing fawners with a weary flourish,
the carp curved, gliding down in soft murk,
jade and amber flicker. From where
my canoe slid on its placid skin
those depths were the better world.
Serene translucent greens
like luminous feathers and shadows
winking mysterious gemlike shimmers.
Yes, quick light stroking
a soft safe place.

As boys during spring flood
we straddled boulders to gig them
or reel their abject sprawl up
on stringed arrows. Mounds of white
buzzing rot stank up the banks.
Some were piebald: orange from Japan
where our five-and-dime-store fish
got spawned or milk white
like the chunks under the leaden scales
bigger than thumbnails that fell off
the hoary old ones we pushed
with sticks in the duck pond.
We heard New York restaurants
fed them to those city scum
as "Cayuga Lake Trout." It was fun
to believe. I remember most
their eyes in those piles,
huge in their gaping heads
and full of nothing, absolutely nothing
like the silence they came from.

Our cottage neighbor, the doctor
in bermuda shorts, stops to talk
about the carp. Fertilizers, nitrates, run-
off, he says. Weeds run riot
in the soup, no bass, just trashy carp.
Every eight words he grimaces horribly
to nudge spectacles up on his nose.
His goggled eyes flash with grace
and happiness. Like a bearer
of bad news to Genghis Khan, let's say,
with one petulant gesture
I could have him slain.

11

Crab in the Hole, Crab in the Hand

for Simone

I can't hear his scrape because the surf
keeps slap-smacking on the heavy sand
and those wheeling birds slice the air
with righteous screeches, but he moves
down there. A few crumbs tremble
on his hole's lip and a grainy rivulet
streams into the abyss. Oh, he's down
there all right: the hermit in his crusted
shell, all bearded and sea-stained.
If I wait long enough an arm will poke
out, elbow first, and maybe a beady
eye on a stalk. That is the way you
behave when everyone wants to eat you.

But I don't eat this kind. At Punta
Sabbione on the Adriatic I grabbed
little scuttlers from the shallows
and tore, two fingers at the eyes,
carapace from abdomen to scoop
out that salty marmalade: crab eggs.
Hands must respect, but never fear
the crabs to do this right. Doubt:
the mildest tremor, will crush shell,
gills, and guts together to disgraceful
trash. Do it or don't, no in-between.

Also, I baited the lighthouse rocks
with rotten squids to catch big crabs,
i granchi. When they darkened
the ghostly moonglow of that meat,
I pulled them up fast to the flagstones
where they clicked and clattered in rage
and terror, I suppose. Who knows
how a creature without heart or brain
must feel? *I* was afraid, because those claws
could really cut, and angry that the *marinaii*
laughed to see my craven hand leap back.

But where am I here? Louisiana.
By a sea again in stiff breeze laden
with kelp and iodine, with memories.
Crab in the hole, crab in the fist;
less real than last week's dream
are the crabs I caught. I cannot wait
for the moon to urge this hermit out.
But I tell you this is not just a hole;
there is a crab down there, breathing small
bubbles in the damp, waiting for night.

Inside the Body

I've knelt on garage cement
and skinned bear. When a fat
black robe lay peeled to its waist,
I suddenly knew those slick bundles!
The Sioux were right; we are the same
tribe under our skins.

The bear's wet-pig smell is really not
unpleasant steaming into dusty rafters:
axle grease and chair batting. A sudden
spill of glistening white intestines,
their slight slither on momentum,
can be a little funny—the same
amusement as to watch a white rump
pump up and down in high weeds,
raising dusts.

And it can feel good to grasp
a slippery store chicken from its plastic
sack, peer up into the cool shadows
of that gothic nave still fragrant
from the guts. I can churn my own
soft tubing in its bone basket
whenever I wish. I rarely say so,
but it feels quite fine to poop.

Each morning I urge my dumb meat
to heave, to flop, and scoot itself
right against her soft side. Happy
snorts greet her in a glitter of sweat
and she knows so well what it wants.
But no single part cares or obeys;
each cell spasms for itself alone.
Each organ constricts to its own purpose.

That was the shock, the fear-pang humming
my spine to buzz my hair roots
as the bear unfolded. The same taste
of bitter metal that dries my tongue-
tip when I am cuckolded. I guess
that tongue's sweet flesh knows
as much of love as the hard-packed
brain and we must cherish what is given
here. I learned that butchering,
not reading Plato who never loved
a woman or skinned a bear.

Hugging

Today many folks talk a big hug
and indeed when they are through with you
you must tuck in your shirt and sigh
several times to feel right. But their eyes
beam everywhere like jacklights
seeking out rabbits and their voices
sound shaped, sweetened like the teacher's
when she asked the janitor for a favor.

We have long suffered the sudden love
of these people. At stoplights, in grocery
stores, even through the walls of our bee-
hive homes they share their music with us.
Singers in such songs are always amazed
at disloyalty and waking sometimes
with some leftover death from our dreams
still in our stomachs they are hard to endure.

On those mornings I want to be hugged.
Very hard. Otherwise I may burst into sorrow
before blossoming bushes. Or full of shame
try to stifle my retching in the toilet stall
knowing their eyes are meeting in mirrors.
On those mornings I don't want just any hug;
I want hers, who smells like herself.

Only she can finger the hairs on my arms
with success. Though they may billow
down on me in perfumed gowns, purring
in their throats with such soft smacking
of lips, their skin is strange to my skin.
So I pray: when my arms open, let them
close only on the warmth of her gift.

The Angry Joggers

Far ahead I spot their gay colors,
maroon and turquoise, emerald
and crimson and I am ashamed
of my slow shamble.
Why, even their shoes are fast streaks
of white light. They seem to swing
the corner of the lake as if the very
air is theirs. So synchronized,
the scenes they leave behind
are tuned aright; some act of physics
tightens the lush morning into sense.
Invisible, one wind flickers the willow
leaves and riffles the water up in edges.
Even my own thick blood seems quicker
as they close on me. I hear rhythmic
breath before I hear it and I step
aside into tangled weeds where snakes
sleep, to stand and receive that rich
waft of energy. But what is this?
Her red, wet face twisted to match
the pitch of furious whine demands
an explanation of his crimes. Eyes
bright as an arsonist's steady
on distant trees; his thin, gray lips
make no reply. And they are past.
As if I was just another blighted bush,
too consumed in themselves to see me,
like the hot, grinding cars on the road,
they have growled by me. I watch
the Rorschach sweat on their shirts
bounce out of sight and then step
back again to birdsongs, a silver fish-
splash, the familiar lap of the lake.

The Gibbon's Hoot

In the bathroom of his former home
he sees the other man's brute whiskers
scummed round the snake-hole drain.

What's to do? Bluff voiced, face stiff
with joy, he buttons the child's coat
and lead-foots it to the zoo.

Ah, she is more delicate, china doll,
each week. Her wren voice woodwinds
up into clear blue where, he thinks,

it becomes pure mathematics and floats
forever—silent. How unlike her sweet
warble are the gibbon's lusty hoots.

Pouches puffed out, roseate, like their red,
− wet peckers in insolent rhythm to and fro
and with the concatenation of their swing,

round and round the square they bang,
bellowing louder and louder from musky
depths and suddenly they stop. So her

small talk, with obscene clamor stopped,
takes again the normal air and sounds so far
away he thinks his heart will break. It won't

though it trebles, *oh god help me, oh
god help me.* Strange knuckles whiten
and gray on the buffalo's chainlink fence.

My eyes are dead, he thinks, but like
cold stars will just see and see for
a million years. He sees her skip

back to him through oblong shadows
of this planet's trees and in disbelief
feels her hand awaken heat in his swollen paw.

Woman Asleep in the Men's Room

for L. Grue

Someone will rape her, or urinate on her,
or both. Not because it is a sinful city
like Paris, or a subconsciously sick city
like London, or a cruel city like Nueva York,
but because it is the thing to do in any city.
What good would it do to guard her sleep
all night, to suffer her piteous whine at dawn?

There is only one way to see New Orleans:
drunk. After a year's sobriety the sun hones
edges sharp and that witches' menstrual blood
called coffee pulls our hearts away, upstream.
Our Lady of the Men's Room dreams this town;
we see it twitch the corners of her mouth,
throb like a bass beneath her purple lids.

Maybe in the dream so deep she will never know
she dreamed it is a hundred years ago and juleps
and oysters are bobbing up iron filigree steps
to where secretly she has just decided to show
her gabled bed to the handsome caller. How
fresh her perfume scents her lacy bodice, under
which her reckless heart trebles like a banjo.

We will leave the money in her yawning purse
and take her dream. We will leave her city,
indifferent to dishonor or virtue. Steady
to the right of the white line, not good jazz
but north country whine fills our car. But,
one breath of cloying rum could whirl us south-
bound against those glaring eyes where Lee,

high on his pillar, guards his sleeping lady.

Dejection at the State U.

for Ralph Adamo

"I pant for life: some good I mean to do,
Despite mine own nature." —Edmund, *King Lear*

The final point, concluded so artfully
that the classbell in its poignant urgency
tones cathartically, is: that Evil really
lives to consume itself and bring forth
mercy in true hearts. We do not believe
it. If we are sinned against or sin our
public words, at first solid as the text
itself, turn to less than vapor in open
air. There is the mind retracing notes in
the dark, amending sight so it will not
interfere with principle or purpose. Cause
is a limited subject, effects lack all con-
viction. Surely we all deserve whipping,
(anyway some do more than others) so
let us do it by rank. Look, a squirrel
is licking moisture from our office window.
We secretly believe in omens, but distrust
metaphor. We must make a list of minds
we do not admire. We must make a list
of minds which pass muster. Otherwise
we will forget. That squirrel has confused
us. Ah yes, here we are in the midst of tenure,
searching promotion, keeping the mind's life
tidy for (alas) an indifferent world already
weary of our quaint amnesia. Who sent
that squirrel, so lean and hungry, anyway?
All the publications in academia could not
extinguish the cruel gleam in his beady eye.
We must hurry to make a list lest we be
found wanting. Let us count our words,
once so slippery—turned to dust, like money
in an old bandanna. And let us root out first
those of few words and blunt honesty whose
simple guise fools us not at all. No sirree.
For it is greatly to be feared that one among
us will soon awake, and all will disappear.

Bareback

Here is a gift of Grace, not just from height
or your proud back—straight for a change,
but, oddly, in this spread-leg vulnerability.

Mostly you admire this miraculous horse,
are honored by the casual shift
of her supple spine, her dignified shimmy.

With the slow sureness of dream
her hooves crush a mixture of spices
from the hazy field swaying

in sunlight. Where quail, meadowlarks
whir up a fanfare for this stately progress
and your heart cannot quell

its beneficence to those wee squeals
of mice, so far below you. Truly
in this sublime posting between clouds

and pastureland, bowing only to the oak
limb, you know again that freedom,
freedom pedestrian equality took away.

Your thighs, her gleaming flanks
are fused in a current of pain,
for could there be joy in this rhythm,

sweet union of sinew and flesh, without ache?
No, you remember a warm throb
from the fly's cruel bite and you crave,

curiously, the bitterness of your mingled sweat.

Horse Sense

I

One after another, down the cement alley
under high dangling bulbs ablaze with halo
but faint light, I threw open their stall screens.
In the darkness I could hear their stamps
and soft splutters as they awoke from green
dreams. At my whistle the sudden rumble
arose, confused crashes from that scramble
shaking the great tin sheets. Cocked
tails flickered up from massive buttocks
into those long faces whose wild nodding
made eyes gleam white arcs for the thunder.

They must have seen a small shadow,
so squat and black in a vast square
of silver heaven as they snorted and chortled
out to me, pushing the smell of horse ahead
of them. And steaming and wheezing on
the frozen yard they rubbed their fat, rough
tongues on my head, jostled me to snow-
banks, nosed me everywhere for fruit
and sugar. Untucked and undone, sprawled in
ice, I was helpless with laughter, too weak
for breath, under their moist, quivering nostrils.

Merry eyes: I was drunk of the whiff of their
sweat, on the rhythmic turmoil of muscle
and hoof. Bright light in the morning.

II

I pole-fished the meadow pond in mid-
summer with my tow-headed children.
Hey, this was supposed to be fun!
But too white and soft for the glare, their
cheeks over-ripened fast and their washed
blue eyes grew lidded from heat and tedium.
The pecan tree, our only shade, fairly
dripped with bitter tannin and from
crushed weeds the still air reeked sweet
and sour with dusts, pollens, chlorophyll
and rank herbal acids. All and everywhere
they touched made an itch, and unseen
but often felt, insects pitched fierce drones.

But it was the horses my kids feared most;
the curious pony who cantered in close
sideways, to grunt and paw the grass.
Sun flashed off his slick flanks and when
he grinned his huge yellow teeth sent
them clutching at my legs, trembling pillars
of a cursed city. Against these woes
their choral whine rose in stridency,
in the face of my disdain, until nothing
remained but to clean the catch and go.

Putting the knifepoint in the black anus
to slice up the milky belly to the throat,
robin's breast/sunrise orange, I glanced
at the small knees grouped around me.
Then higher into a silent gaze of disgust.
Their eyes on my sequined, gory hands
were as blank as when they recoiled from
The viscous saliva roping the old mare's
mouth. Too small to phrase it for themselves;
I asked instead: Was this cruelty born in me
or did I learn? It is long past memory.

I led my wife's children around the mines
of mahogany turds, back to the baking car.

III

On famous Bourbon Street I saw old nags
hooked to tourist buggies, parked in full
sun. Yellow mucus dripped from slack
mouths to the recycled cobbles of that
adult disneyland for deviants, and often
I saw fetlocks matted with oozing scabs
and flies preening their resplendent faces
in a paradise of open sores. Too humid
for prolonged rage, too overwhelmed
by sordid sight to pity any but myself,
I hid in the ersatz cool of an unlit bar.
Even there I heard the driver croak "Ya-
hoo!" and that forlorn clop-clop
fade into city sounds like memories
ringing back so vague you feel the cells
give a final pop and give up sense for good.

My father tended a horse like that.
While his father quoted scripture
by the hour to customers, he sat
on the wagon seat, lost in great books.
That patient beast knew the route,
the way home, and how to stamp
for oats. My father's body sat sentry
over the inventory, while his mind
stormed Troy, or led white Bucephalus
out of a cool glade onto Persian plains.

Like a Gift this vision, more real than
the cruel streets, took me in the Absinthe Bar:
Father high on his perch in brown knickers,
his eyes drinking the words, the slightest
twitching of lips, while around the whole cast
glowed a profound calmness of horse.
And I arose from the untasted whiskey,
eager for the road, eager for new pastures
where horses browsed in shadows of oil tanks.

Talking with Animals

Bird brains really *can't* shelve a single thought,
so catbirds natter the same old song
all morning long. By high noon,
when live oak leaves are lacquered almost black,
what's said ceases to be worth the saying.
So they.stop, but I'm half convinced
the hound dogs bay all night for pure song
alone. The way Keats loved the bell-dirge
of "forlorn" on a humid night, or how
the black man's blues hop us up to dance.
As a lad, I began too seriously to chat
with animals, but now I cajole, speechify,
and just outright coo to their guileless eyes,
lush, lolling tongues. And they talk back.
Among us, we listen to others for our own
sounds, but with these others we are singers
singing for the sweet sound's sake
and our tails (our happy, happy tails)
wag joyous beats, strong hearts never missing.

Black Cat

The half-Siamese are often all black
like bright coal, a rainbow petrol sheen
winking in the sun off shoulder tips
and swinging stomach. This cat is only
a fierce hunter of dead leaves and one-
legged crickets, but his sleek passage
suggests a more brutal mystery. Plutonic
stalker across our lush lawns; jays
and catbirds see Death's Shade and from
safe boughs shrill "Shame Thief, Shame!"

His up-turned gaze seems serene
but inside his eyes, as through mica,
I see languid sulphur swirls, green
and yellow flames spitting from
a seething mass. I remember an old bite
wound on his haunch: how the wet meat
blazed out of the black in hot reds
and oranges. I think the birds agree
he is a volcanic thing. Evil parades
as beauty, often in the light of day.
He looks tamed to half-lidded decadence
in my blonde daughter's lap—
I am not fooled by his gentle rumble.

He reminds me of the forest's deepest
shadows, so quietly they start
a relentless slide over scrub and clearing
to the hearth itself. Like the Devil
himself smelling of peculiar smoke,
but shoulder to shoulder with sable deacons
in draughty pews. While a bat flaps
across the moon, a blind white newt
creeps far below in the cave's dew.
As my mind feels its way deeper into
the darkness, the black cat rolls
his back in the swingset's dust
and grim birds screech from highest limbs.

A Surreal Snake

In wintertime when the king snake sleeps
the deepest possible sleep, a faintest
hiss in his blood like a pilot flame's
least flicker, then you might find him
coiled in the woodpile's last logs.
Your prodding twig wouldn't stir him.
So you might balance his stiff loops
on a firmer stick to catapult him
treetop high against the close, gray sky.

At the apex of that fling, you might
see him waken, straighten and re-knot.
Missing the fluid grip of muscle to dirt,
he would thrash like a snapped chain
whipping wild off an engine block.
But this terror would be silent;
his scream is too high-pitched for you.
Only a towhee's invisible scratch
under rhododendron might fill the instant.

Also the sound of your chuckle.
A private joke about the word "gravity"
might billow in your gut and cheeks.
The king snake would glide off unstunned
into jimson straw, his bright tongue
needling air for the taste of heat.

Prose Poem About a Horse

When families get together, at the tables' far corners
there is always one old man who if he could remember
would tell such fine tales! Deaf, mute, ignored,
he gums what soft food he can and I, least welcome
guest, most distant relation, am always seated
next to him. At these tables talk is always the same:
business, divorce, ailment, and death. But this old one
and I have no choice but to concentrate on the plates
set before us. Particularly him, for if given the chance
I will steal his sweet giblets, spoon into his custard.
How we love that steaming mountain lake of brown
gravy in the mashed potatoes! New peas glisten
with butter and we can gnaw rich juices from the skin.
After eating, the old man twists his head to tell
me his one story. Ready for it again I study his shock
of white hair, fine as new corn tassel, his powder-soft
flesh. But I can never see his eyes; instead the long
table of feasters looms back in his eyeglasses. Fat
women are fatter with chasmic cleavages, thin ones
curve in fantastic bows. You should see those
huge mouths, lips gleaming with grease, teeth
flashing gold and silver. The story is always
the same: about a horse long ago who knew
quitting time and the way home and he tells
it loud, the old voice vigorous with wonder.
He bangs his bony palm on his bony knee.
I suspect moisture from regret and joy wells
in his eyes, but of course I can only nod and smile
to my distended self where we could have met without
words. Sometimes he shows photos the color of underdone
turkey: those dappled forms could be horses, or fingerprints,
or ancient grime on barn walls. I reflect on this story,
its possible wisdom through long afternoons before sand-
wiches, in smoky rooms with blocked corners where men
howl at football over whiskey and no pretzels. Hearty Uncles
always pummel my arm, squeeze my bones.
"Getting ideas for your writin' from old granpa? Havin'
a good time? Fine. Fine!" Vast caverns of air fill
their chests, oxygen hisses from their musk-rimmed pores.
Yes, I always say to the great spaces they leave,
I love that story when I have eaten well. It is a beautiful
story about a horse with special intuition and kindness
who is now dead after many years of faithful service,
but not forgotten. Whenever this story is told our family
swells with pride, and it is always new.

Poem from the Study by the Interstate

Its constant threnody is ceaseless
exhalation—an eternal sigh,
but big rigs pass with a sustained
snarl, solo moans rising above
the background dirge. I even hear
the rhythmic whack of pebbles
buried in the treads. The driver,
weary from hours of dull jounce
and solitary thought, does not hear
himself so loud. The motor purrs
for him, and those hot cylinders
just whine. As I am used
to a bitter mildew smell here
from my rug, he thinks his commotion
is the universe's normal roar.

This Sunday morning I also hear
perfect matins toll from the loudspeaker
of some distant church. Thin brick
veneer, no doubt, with cinderblock
behind. Closer, a bluejay's low-class
vulgarity obtrudes and beneath this shed
a squirrel scrapes like a rat in pecan
leaves. Is there purpose in his search,
I wonder? Or like my mind, do his paws
scrabble detritus for any solid chunk
to hold? Brute clamor shudders the pencil
poised over the writing page. A slough of oak
leaves falls through my open door like
rigid little corpses. Winter comes
with its grinds and whines, parting air
for the cold, white silence.

Hunting Agates at Big Creek

for Michael Colvin

How it soothes me to sit still a long time
by cold waterflow over cold stones;
to look very hard for a long time
at a small place, learning nothing.
But if I did not throw up my head
sometimes to suck in quick a new gout
of chill air it would be no good.

There it all is: atop the loamy cut
great pines joined in looming shadow
against sea-blue with its wistful trace
of cloud. And its one crow,
never in a hurry, flapping down the breeze
dead center in the stream's vast fairway.
Over dunes' undulant ridges,
soft hummocks and hollows, taluses
of bright chert and ancient coral-chalk
that suddenly whack to life as the killdeer
beats out of the swales. His white bobber
skims in tune with a little jig of wavelets
in shallow rapids and is a speeding gleam
ghosting the log-jammed pools.

The melancholy of these shades is sweet only
beneath a brilliance of lacquered green.
That it all stays still under a wide sky
is good to know as my eyes strain
square feet for agates. I see lozenges
of rosy quartz, limestones gouged
and stream-polished to sensual plaintiveness:
my thumb rubs and rubs as if for luck.
Also conglomerates: pyrogenic loops and coils
from chthonic flames are in frozen meander
through countryrock. Just-plain-holes
suddenly become intricate sea-whorled fossils
lit by a wink of adjacent geode sparkles.

All that and more is there in happy jumble,
but today I only pocket agates.
A rule firmly based on whim, options
always open including the choice to change
it all. I could empty these beauties
to the stream and, head high, legs
limber, follow the flight of the crow.

Peckerwoods

"What-what-what-Cheer?" is what I decided
the cardinal said, a gaudy clarion bright
as virgin's blood, trilling from a fir tree's
peak. We were pleased to think our pathetic
whistles fooled him, gave him cause to sing.

So turning the trail's bend, we were outraged,
soul-sickened, to see peckerwoods sweep the last
swirling paper bits from their pickup's bed.
It palled our serene communion. Peckerwoods:
William Percy's word, said with stiff-lipped

patrician distance for drifting human trash.
Snopes, we literary *cognoscenti* get
from Faulkner, but those are clever.
I think the bird name comes from a shock
of tameless, greasy hair tufting

a bucktoothed, hatchet head, sometimes limp
across a sallow brow. Of course, the flat crack
of that up-river twang and careless violence
of peckers' cruel beaks could contribute.
We saw grimy children toss up rakes and brooms

and scramble up aboard. We watched the truck
lurch off over roots and ruts, leaving a stink
of blue haze behind. By the time we reached
their ugly, jumbled litter, sparrows already
hopped and pecked through that rich bonanza.

Their happy cheeps harmonized with the wind's
calm sough through pines. A thicket of vines
seemed to be already coiling tin cans,
paper, and plastic shreds down in toward
the forest floor. But our mood was wrecked;

we talked of how they sometimes light
the trash to hide its trace, or from sullen
hatred of the *posted* signs. "Torch these woods
where we're tossed to rust," we thought they think.
And that eldest girl: despite the jouncing blur,

we'd seen defiance flame in her blue eyes, as pretty
and spirited now as she'd ever be. We decided she'd
be married by sixteen. What a waste, we sighed
and sighed again. For it is a lonely burden
to own a tender heart that knows all things.

Cedar Waxwings in Ligustrum Lucidum

for Philip Dow

Two hundred waxwings! Swarming on berry bunches
like bees to a comb, bats on a cave ceiling.
Their greedy thrashes flounced branchlets
every which way so the tree looked palsied
with panic—or ecstasy? We focused on each
soft brown squirm flashing small bursts
of wild yellow. Each bird was stemmed
in cluster by a single clawhold, batting
for balance—furious beaks jabbing for fruit.

All shrill cheeps rose above a whir of wings
like a dread locust whine into one vast vowel
scream. They whipped their own wind up
and catbirds wheeled around shrieking *Sin!*
Sin! Like prophets raging to heedless revelers.

Though I warbled by your side my single
preacher's hymn, pagan joy must have surged
your pulse. You are keen-eared to Nature's
unbroken hum and in some good solitude
can raise the rush again. So your poem
chants in pre-Roman tongues—sweet gutturals
tiding blood to the head, sprouting tears
as salty as the sea the first light tasted.

Because I always search for lessons,
particularly in trees, I saw the sin
of Gluttony, an orgy of Public Drunkenness.
I frowned at the downcast gaze of a child
on wobbly rollerskates trudging through
the ligustrum shade. I shook my head
at bright traffic flashing the sunlit streets.

Why such a dour sulk? A mash of roots
and berries once relit mysteries in my brain.
Strangers' voices leapt from my own mouth;
pale visions sleeping in my genes woke
as omens in my dreams. But I tell you Philip,
I fear a kind of sigh-wracked sleep
when ghosts, soft and brown, flutter down
the nether mind to crowd air from my lips.
In full daylight I felt a sudden squeeze
when waxwings gorged on the ligustrum tree.

The Mississippi River at Baton Rouge

for C. deGravelles

Can you remember when the air just smelled
like pine trees, wet dirt, a few flowers?

Worlds on worlds still tumble over
and this river which was always muddy
retains its surface sparkle.
But only a fond heart builds immortal
faith on a few bright bubbles.

Look here: to dig a dirt pit,
the Rodesto Brothers have snapped off
a mile of full-grown poplars to our thigh-
level with some dreadnought machine.
Dynamite comes next, but for now several
songless robins puff feathers fat
against unbroken wind, hunched on stumps
above the slurry. And look there:

across the "Father of Waters" where
the real South sits like a white and silver
city, mysterious in a lavender mist.
From its stacks spectacular blasts
of greasy dragon flames roll up
the blackest funeral smoke, relentless
as our planet's tumble into night.
This catfish at our feet, body picked
to mush by gulls, gapes a mouth full
of oily sand. My finger flicks on my hand
like the tail of a nervous wren; my tongue
muscles out gray words for the gray air.

Does the river's profound and solemn flow
tug some deeper, more ancient, current
in our blood than the pale resignation
of this age can stir? Let's talk
of Shelley's death; no one today
would press your own great heart in a book.
You are a Strong Swimmer, but I have seen
where a tossed match would not hiss out
but flared gem-green on the water's skin.

To insist this water is fit for baptism,
that arcadian spirits dart and swarm
above this bloated fish, could insult
true friendship that still endures
in the dusty light, dim vapors
of this shore. Our river will soon vault
these flimsy levees and with one world's spin
twist free in its wild thirst for salt.

Speaking of Sounds

for Holley Galland

So you like that muffled echo, like a runlet's
faraway drizzle into a cavern's inky pool,
which is the steeped coffee's little fall
in the pot? And the puc-a-puc-a-puc-a
of plastic sprockets in a toy car—you like
that too? Saying so makes me recollect

my rod's slicing whistle, the line's soft hum
running deep for moments into the mist,
and the distant splash. Then just the scrape
of a thrush behind me. In that pond
bass struck by the reel's third revolution,

or not at all. Those poor fish, their last
sullen thumps in the ice-chest
were likely ghostly hands burrowing in coins
and jewels. Their wet, gray flesh was firm
and they did not want to die. Dream-

sounds, perhaps variations of the buried
bloodbeat, surface in tranquillity. Press
a finger on your lidded eye so inner suns
glare forth. On the final flicker of those
flames, memory of light, our final terror rests.

But for now the concussive throb on your
fingertip is almost sound itself. Almost
a pop and hiss of gases flaring in wet wood.
Two beady eyes, flames steady in each core,
rustled up dead leaves beyond the waver
where my cooking fire gave up against the night.

Beneath the rhythmic scratch I thought I heard
a restless heart, like mine but smaller, quicker.
I thought I had a spirit, because it hungered.

The Physics of Yellow

for R. Haymaker

Each bubble has its own wind inside
blowing against the tumble of that skin
of water, and thus against the weather
of the universe. So friction from both
sides bursts beer bubbles I imagine
rise from my slack mouth to hover
in the bar of sun from the filthy window.

Smoke, beer, piss, and pine-sol:
all these smells are the color yellow.
Yellow weather of tropic sirocco
whirls in my bubbles, which ascend
in that arid, yellow shaft. Ellipsoid,
the yellow room revolves on the slick
globes, a lighter yellow in the heat.

When the phone rings a billion yellow
bubbles jump from my startled flesh.
Someday I will be nothing, like the space
where a bubble was. But everywhere will be
my stain. Bands of yellow surround
our world and from where I lounge
on its surface, giving freely of my gases,
yellow is the color of all matter.

Concert Time

We know some friction
or concussion always makes it:
hairs rubbing dried guts,
or rub of air squeezed hard
through coiling tubes, or felt-
tipped hammers on taut wires
tapping. But what can words
say of it? I mean our love
of it. Brains hold shapes
long after earbones cease
to tremble. So we know
a little; we can talk
about it. That is not enough.

Once a very real thing filled
all the air, made certain moves
for a certain time. I saw you
close your eyes to not see it
made, only what it was and did.

We did talk after with nouns,
verbs, all those parts. But it
was over. We wished words
to shape the same for each,
for my voice to form in you
as yours in me. My eyes
were open, dear; I can picture
what was really there.
Beyond that, you said, I heard
what was really meant.

What is the use?
A sudden flurry of white balls
pummeling the kettledrums—
that copper blaze
in the stagelight's golden
smear struck me then.
A measured rise of thunder
roll argues louder now.
Shapes collect in no single
use. Like those colored lights
I hear behind your lidded eyes.

"Grown Quiet at the Name of Love"

"Adam's Curse," W. B. Yeats

Each sunrise, I rise:
to watch cobalt redden at its edges,
sometimes scarlet as a berry stain
or more purple like a fading bruise.
The moon's still there, much smaller
in its placid shimmer than older moons
we've seen, but still very high, old
and lovely in its dwindle. And some
mornings I wake with some grand old
lines of poetry lingering from dreams,
still ready on my tongue. Love poems,
in the rare, high quaver the masters
made when they made love to beauty.

The three spinal links that arc are always
stiff from the long night's drift
in the too-soft mattress of our bargain bed.
House air smells sour, because we've sucked
and sighed it through ourselves
all night, so I pad out
into all that cold-beaded sparkle,
fresh hunger of bluejays, to breathe
new air and coffee steam,
to loosen meat and bones.

Morning resembles paradise:
the first few sunbeams fire the dew
in thatched St. Augustine; down through
layers of sweetgum, live oak, willow,
pecan, camphor, one million light
green hearts of chinese tallow
these new shafts bounce and spill out.
This early I don't mind the jay's raw
brass, those shrill assertions
of their rights. Their vulgar screams
are just comic counterpart to deep sunlit
peace that keeps the butterfly afloat.

Each morning, I keep half my thoughts
for you, still dreaming in our curtain-
shadowed room, puffed soft and smelling
of sweet slumber. I think you're beautiful
and I still keenly love you
even after all the weary-hearted years,
though our ways have grown so far apart
it seems sometimes we only share
the sunshine bobbing motes between us.
At a sudden flood of rising sun,
the jaybirds cease at once and gentler
chatter takes the brightened day.
At that hour, it doesn't seem so bad,
this silence around my echoing head.

Silent Treatment

I heard you say "mills of justice,"
but choosing not to fully focus
on your voice, I let windmills
slide firm and clear, bloom colors
in the darkness of my head.
Not those broad Dutch blades,
crossed and tilted above more tulips
than the eye can tighten on,
but our own wide-awake daisies
purring or clanking lonely high on
straight derricks above bare dust
and, comically, the wind which grinds
and grinds that dust against bleached
and browning boards. Your metaphor
meant stones of course—millstones,
our native cromlechs. A real one
I know lies like a heavy, granite
doughnut, half-sunk in johnson grass.
Ladies stepped from it into carriages,
but the house and drive have completely
disappeared. What do they do
with all those tulips? What matters is
I should have listened to how you meant,
"The mills of justice grind slow, yet
exceeding fine," to mean. Now,
your humid pout has stopped some music
I took for granted, like wind and water.
Something dusty in your reason
made me wink inward, to stare too hard
at bright pebbles I could push in patterns
in my head. I admit this wrong.
Please speak to me, so I can stop
this dull focus on this lonely moment;
set free my mind to dance for you,
this time for you.

Dr. Holmes Observes Melville for Signs of Insanity

for J. Babin

"Our good Herman's remarks are not often cheerful;
would you drop by, ostensibly for tea, to observe
possible pathology?" But the jolly doctor, Oliver
son of Abiel, was weak on those who really chose
their Greeks, and would not with surety diagnose.

Was this learned confrontation an early skirmish
in our long war between the lost and the found?
Actually, these men conversed around the theme
in tactful sympathy—both knew very well that chill,
not from cracks, but the deacon hanging in the vestibule.

You might think Melville would resent a hack
who published all his prattle as if Homer's lordly art
was for nothing but a chuckle at the breakfast table.
But perhaps Holmes began like this: "Infection, never seen,
is spread by hands and instruments which are not clean

though they appear pristine. I wish our fellow citizens
would heed that wisdom from my pen." And maybe
Herman Melville said: "Your happy work exudes
a confidence which lullabyes knavishness for fools;
I beg your pardon, the moderate man can be Evil's tool."

"But Herman, doesn't the good man catch more flies
with honey?" "Excuse me, I speak of words not condiments,
and why lure game you would not eat with such exotic
bait? Listen doctor, I have heard in a South Sea gale
that same mid-sermon pitch that made our devils wail."

At this, no doubt, the water got too deep for Dr. Holmes.
Storms? Devils? "Though this be madness, yet there
is method in't," he might have quoted at leave-taking,
puffing to the eye-level of haggard Melville women.
Europe was then anodyne for New England madness;
Italian sun alfresco for our stern and wintry genius.

Each family views its writers with dismay.
Whether they strut our griefs to thunderous applause,
or glower in attic solitude while the whole house echoes
a screeching pencil; their words become too pure to share,
like the eternal pledge of love that was never really there.

You Had to Know Her

For a long time she listened to the sound
of Leo waving his arms. Then as she listened
she began listening to a few carefully chosen
other things and gradually she called these sentences.
Soon she was seeing what it seemed others were not seeing
that these ones were a lot like talking and talking was sounding
like thinking and if one could be thinking it why should one be doing.
So she stopped listening
and did what Leo was not doing with his thinking.

I'm sorry. There is no other way to describe
it. I'm describing what cannot be described
because she said it all when she said it.

Once you spent all day Christmas taking
apart and putting together a puzzle
from Formosa. Your headache was special,
had nuance that night and your tantrum
was misunderstood. Over-tired and over-
excited they said, but you had just learned
the best moments would never be enough.

Miss Stein not interested in your problem.

Let's not get confused; like Mallarmé
you had to know her beautiful voice, her jig-
saw salon: that museum for the talking.
She loves your worry, your tender buttons,
half your words; she just don't like your
story. "I very recently met a man who said,
how do you do. A splendid story," she said.

O.K., good-bye.

Winter 1910: Bateau Lavoir, Paris

That winter in the Bateau Lavoir
it got too cold to fight.
I'd come back to our filthy room
(she never cleaned!)
to catch her blue hands cupping
flames from my burning sketches.
I was just too tired and chilled
to hit her. But I took money
her mother sent, bought paints
and painted her blue and jagged.

I learned to daub fast,
she so soon turned white
like dirty marble, and shook.
Billowing steam from my yelling
when she shivered gave me vision.
I made a bull with beautiful nostrils.

She whimpered in her sleep,
belched sour gas in a corner
when the fat Yank dressed
like a man came to buy.
I think she slept with the poet
downstairs for biscuits. Ah,
it was hard but the work was good.

That was later. One night I saw
my hand in the gaslight. Gone
were the slender olive fingers.
These were square, thick, and ruddy
and I was so pleased. You know
that buttock, golden as a ripe
pear, its warm rosy light?
What *ampleur!* That was her
before the cough made her skinny.

A Normal Man

To birds what looks like a viceroy could be
a nasty monarch. Beyond sweet and sour
our world is smelled. These are school-
boy facts, but to chew each morsel
thirty-two times is to savor an illusion,
a "philosophy of life." Since I know well
real Guilt, undeniable as a heart attack,
this gas-pain remorse on a rainy day
is counterfeit. Henri Matisse could use

his weak eyes, his very sensible brain,
to show us a new truth in a blue hat.
It is mighty blue. Nor is there much depth
in his red room which is not an angry home,
just very red. "Tell the American people
that I am a very normal man who enjoys
raising flowers," he said. How touching
that this was not normal for my countrymen.

As a schoolboy, learning facts of words,
figures, and hygiene, I thought all hard ideas
would get clear, like getting used to ammonia
stench in the hallways. It was like the henhouse,
but never, I repeat, *never* have I confused
the big words with chicken waste. Nothing
is clear and still inside I feel anxious shame.

Only when the cardinal, so very red,
flutters down to the puddle do I notice
what a green place this is. Matisse also did that.
When many smart ones saw it and made it
smart the knot inside him loosened.
If you have such a knot you can tell.

Each morning I must sit with the empty page
and wait for a new mystery to pass through
me. Soon so much comes, the tastes, colors,
voices in the steady blood, I am tied tight.
This is not normal. It is a little better
than that to love this life, which loves no one.
Of course Matisse once knew that.

Still Life

Three yellow wasps belly crawl by slow feel
over boulders of black ripe cherries
in a blue china bowl. Their bands stripe
even blacker against the sun color
as they crouch to split skin, curl down
to the lavish gore. That sugary pulp
blazes crimson, royal purple and pink—
as bright as a brass horn's highnote.

I've jammed wet brushes under many eaves,
but wasps let me be. My stink is right
or wrong, I guess. But I don't go stabbing
them with rolled papers or coffee cans
either, when they do their buzz-bounce dance
off walls and window panes. I can peer close
to see their feelers stroke, so very slow,
as they suck. Because I fidgeted for years

in chalky rooms and twirled home, light after
yellow light, smashed on the brain-busting Grace
of a girl's smell still on my clothes, I can
half-doze this instant into hours. My voice
once stormed all night like candy colored lights
kids bang off the walls to help their minds race
wild. It's luck to smell good or bad, to still
be here with a brain jampacked with old noise

and color. So still now sleeping in soft folds,
dark wrinkles where each yellow thought creeps
feeling the way slow, sure, and alone.

Confessional for Police

When I saw those legs, soaked denim,
rigid in a cold morning rain,
I thought nobody passes out that hard.

And I should know.

When I saw those legs up close:
Dr. Scholl's shoes dogcrap brown,
ruby socks poking from the Volkswagen's
dim catacomb, I knew what we had here
was a murder.

Because that black man's brains (whiter
than I remembered!) speckled vinyl
and one chunk lay like tapioca
in cherry syrup.

Man? Hell, he wasn't near eighteen.

When the cop drove his flashing unit
up (more red and white for visuals)
he was not a philosopher. But let
me tell you something; nor am I.
When that stiff's wrist alarm buzzed
off we both jumped just as high.
And laughed; we laughed the same
laugh. Heh-heh-heh—like that.

The park behind my backyard
where we two stood in sullen rain
and mud, just us two in full sniper-
view, is a long way from your neighborhood.

Listen, that isn't true, forgive me.
I am a little bit upset lately.

Numb toes blues: slow motion
stomp, shoulders in the buzzard
hunch and both of us knew
unsaid, unseen, inside his shoe too
they gray and pucker.

If I must continue this cliché
of violence ("*parce que je suis fou*,"
as Nijinsky answered Diaghilev)
it should be for police
who also drink coffee all night
and wear their griefs on their hips,
instead of you. Tell me pal,
entre nous, is Saint Genêt *passé*?

My statement: One muggy August eve,
seventeen years before, I beer-bottled
a drunk trucker's eye in Whitney Point,
New York. *Caveat emptor.*
I'd do it again.

A smoldering log just crashed off
my heart in a shower of sparks.

Ah, that is full-moon monkeyshine
to suck toxic brainlobes up too hard
against their pans. "Love or Die,"
who really struck that axiom?
With rigor I have lived a third
alternative, but would now, shyly,
welcome

change.

Fire Rain

At first its thunder booms far-off, here
and then there like duck hunters or old battles
fought on real fields or even in the towns.
They prayed in bed then while their city burned.
But with a sudden Bang it's beside us: *il pleut*—
same old rain on the town in the heart and so on.
The gray splatter into its fallen self.
Our English word sounds French for queen
or nothing, but brighter like the green drip
shining in steamy after-blaze.

Tonight's rain shushes down hard outside
on poplar leaves that would twirl in gusty rain.
We eat fish at formal dinner and some talk
of death in air, water, earth—everywhere
and also cooking fish and children. Without
true listening it drums and patters like rain
on layers of black humus. It's so pleasant
to recollect Verlaine, a tang of chestnut tannin
after a spring shower. *Sur la ville, dans mon
coeur* etcetera. And as a boy I once stood

by a streaming window holding sports equipment
or someone's hand, I can't remember, but now
the waiting, for cancer I guess, seems so
different. What's this acid smoke burning
in each icy drop? And why does this woman say
her child's too smart to act polite or play
with "average" kids? Did Boccaccio's gentlefolk
gab like this at dinner, the stench of burning
dead well behind them in their city? Maybe
it's not sad their young are fat on gaseous whine,

otherwise sorrow might sear our love to ashes.
There! That there is bitter rain gushing hard,
sudden and straight down the heart's gutters.
Sour rain, each drop aflame, that should be tears—
les larmes to soothe a face fanned red with shame.
O anger, it is all pity wrung from fear
to flash and boom in my heart on the town
in my heart until the sweet rain sighs down.
In the candle's drop of fire I saw the lake
of fire we'll step to in a final rain of fire.

Like crabs rose-blooming in kettles of fire
our arms will open to embrace what hisses
up from our hearts on fire. Ah hell, water
or fire, please let this beating rain wash clean
on the darkened wood and blackened town.

Letter to a Cousin on His Twentieth Deathday

I

After weeks of tasks, petty chores for petty gains,
I want to write like Milton did. Some vast music
well beyond cluttered sight should swell my heart,
engage this hand to inspired scribble. Or at least
in the language of real men I would speak for your ears
only, seemingly, of what it is to be thirty-six
in these last decades of human age. Oh, I hear a song
all right and have learned to let it soar, or murmur
low inside my skull. But the words are prose,
calm prose at best. You are dead today for twenty years
and I heard you say once when you lived you held
no faith with another life. Nothing there but unimaginable
nothing. My secret is: for twenty years I wrote
words, not for moonlit lovers embraced in single-
minded squirm, but for all you dead. For I imagine
not nothing but everything where you are, that you
can hear music that I meant beyond the labored scrawl.

II

If so, you may recall the old Crew Club
at Cornell where you took me one full-moon night
with two college girls and Mr. Boston gin. It was pink
gin, I think, and it burned like pepper in my throat—
so sweet, so hot, yet fresh as chewed pine needles in the nose.
I still cannot reason why at nineteen you let all that go.
Right there in half-light stinking of jocksweat and canvas,
right in front of us under tiers of rowing shells, you coupled
with the prettiest girl. Her white (so white!) thighs
billowed beneath your thrusting like phosphorescent jellyfish
that ghost in night-black seas. You chided me for being shy,
for not grappling with the homelier one in a parody of love.
The truth is: your girl was the second ugliest girl
God ever made and mine smelled like a wet civet.
That was not it. Without your prodigious pants, hoarse
cries of joy, you could have heard my breath whistle
like wind through a chink in a dry cave.

III

Last August, on my yearly visit home (I am not
undutiful), I drove Mother to the farmers' market.
To step across slurred wheel ruts rimmed with weeds
spiked wretchedly askew, Mother had to clutch that loose

wattle of flesh on my arm. I am middle-aged, Cousin;
our small mothers look so alike by now you would
look hard to know your own. Her dry fingers dug so deep
a birdlike tremble from her bum heart passed into me.
Once as she rested, I glanced back at Ithaca Inlet
and there in solemn waver on its placid skin loomed
our old Crew Club. And of course I remembered.
Like lightning I remembered. For many years I have not
seen your face that clear, that wild grin. And blood
in my groin got quick and talked through some secret
streams to blood in my brain. My nose filled again
with giddy mollusk-stench of sex, and my poor heart;
it bulged tight in my chest like a fat melon left to split.
Teeth set in misery, glaring hard into those sepia-tint,
jigsaw splashes of hometown sky at my feet, I asked
what I have not asked for many years: why did you leave
me alone in this sad place? You son of a bitch.

    IV

In this life which you chose to leave on your brother's
motorcycle, selfish to the end, even our most cherished
outrage passes. As I led mother down the vendors' midway,
I wondered what you would think of those "farmers,"
poet-bearded and ponytailed, some already half-sedated
before noon on their real cash crop. You, who did not even
live to see beatniks fade into freaks. One free spirit
scooped gobs of pale honey with two fingers from a jar
hand-labeled "Natural." He let it drip to his open mouth,
wide as a baby bird's, while around his russet beard buzzed
a score of delighted flies. I watched his slitted eyes
watch for my disgust. To be invisible I still wear
the majority's plain uniform we wore over twenty years
ago, when you came to my parents' house for Sunday
dinners. It was always roast beef, always almost raw,
and those potatoes' insides crunched like apples.
You were to tutor me through Cicero, I think,
but often we sneaked off to drink the stars to sleep
where Cayuga Lake lapped declensions more eternal
against the shale-pebbled shore. Hating that slob
behind my poker face, instead of you, I let the fish-
breeze of that lake cool my face, and I let my senses
recollect cold smoothness in those lozenges.

51

V

A living mind can do so many things at once.
What if none delight, if only one dread circumstance
looms above the rest? Milton said that when they mate
in heaven, *they merge completely*. I do not think
you knew that, but I know I saw you try it once.
And I wonder how this prose transposed in lines,
these words sucked up so fast by this planet's air,
sound as music in your angelic head? In twenty years
I will write again, perhaps in notes, to let
you know what I have managed to forget.

What Springs to Life

Funny how I remember colors
because the TV was black and white.
Martin Luther King and his friends were pushed
close together by a gremlin ring of faces
from Breughel, or Goya, or even MAD magazine.
I'd swear to a rich mocha-brown, but dark gray
was the truth and the red sweaty faces just gray.
Someone's socks glaring under highwater jeans
were white as hell. King's flat face was taut
from fear, but his voice breathed old-gold deep
and steady. "At this moment our brothers'
killers walk free in this city." And someone
jeered, "Standin right behind you, nigger!"
I never saw that faceless mouth at all,
but I'm sure it was a smile as thin and raw
and purple as an infected cut. This thing
truly happened, but even if it hadn't
it should have for its terror and the pity.

Like that poem where the banana company's
colonel dunks his victims' severed ears
in his water glass: that feels more true
than fact. Dried ears should spring to life
like boxed apricots instead of floating high
and brown on the water's skin for at least
a day, always bobbing from the pencil's thrust.
What truth springs from a gradual gray bloat?
A slowmotion drift flaking like quiet tedious
dandruff in dreamy somersaults down the glass
sides through the gray water to soft sleep,
a putrid white sediment? Or when Cocteau
put a mouth on the palm of a hand and then
the hand with those puckering lips crept
down to the groin, that seemed so right too.

Before Cocteau got shown in our town, the kids
got put on these tracks. The gifted ones
learned about Greeks and different ways to think
the truth, while us average kids learned facts
so we could do our work without needless worry.
I read all the books anyway, just for the hell
of it. So when I walked downtown with my pal,
Bill Smock, to the new movie every Saturday night,

I could talk some about the truth instead
of just cars and we sang folk songs: "Michael
rowed the boat ashore . . ." Our song words sprang
out as solid gray clouds because we meant them
with all our hearts and I think the pinprick
stars and the moon, so skinny and faraway
like a clipped fingernail, got us just a little
crazy. That's why on February first, 1958,
we stopped and turned back from our own gray faces
ghosting in the glass over the licorice, back
into that blackness sweet from spilled soda
for the second show of *The Seventh Seal*.
We'd thought *Seal* would be seal, as in Flipper,
and we were nuts for Alan Ladd in *Robin Hood*,
but for the first time truth whispering in books
had sprung to life, and then to colors in our heads.

I guess we looked pretty silly
in our town. Our little liberal lights thrilling
for montage, modern art, and the workers' paradise.
We loved Martin Luther King and hated the men
who hated him with a fiercely sad and joyous
righteousness that sprang from our hearts
just like love. I have no excuses.
For a long time I thought I was on the wrong
track. I worried at my work and in my sour bed
that my heart was drowned in brine or withered.
Which, I didn't know. But the factual truth is,
love was always there, waiting to spring to life.
We'd loved King's dream because we yearned
like a thirst inside for our country's love
to bloom again like Shelley's heart: plucked
from fire, dried and pressed until it sprang
to life in a rain of tears. So when the Nam vet
showed me the withered ear from his wallet, shyly
like a condom, on the Greyhound in the middle
of both the black night and the country,
I wasn't shocked. I'd seen a whole pouch spilled
on a Baton Rouge bar. We were both just average
and I knew the ear, matter of fact in his hand,
would never spring to life. And he knew that.
Our faces were both gray in the black window
and I saw in his eyes the truth in his heart
and I was honored by his terror and the pity.